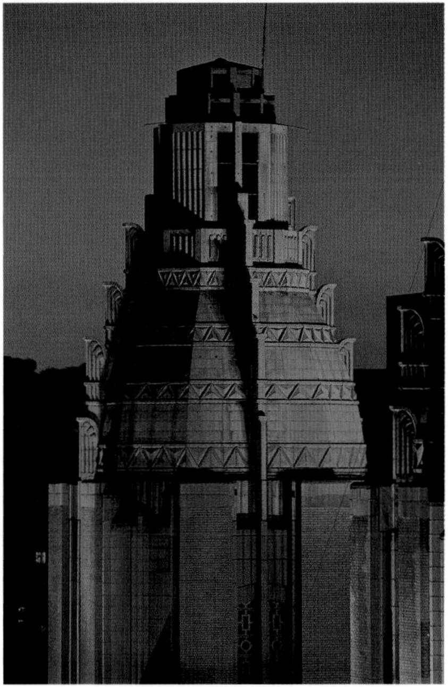

RIZZOLI
NEW YORK

New York · Paris · London · Milan

RICHARD BERENHOLTZ

NEW YORK

NEW YORK

FOREWORD BY KENNETH T. JACKSON

A WELCOME ENTERPRISES BOOK

RIZZOLI INTERNATIONAL PUBLICATIONS, INC.

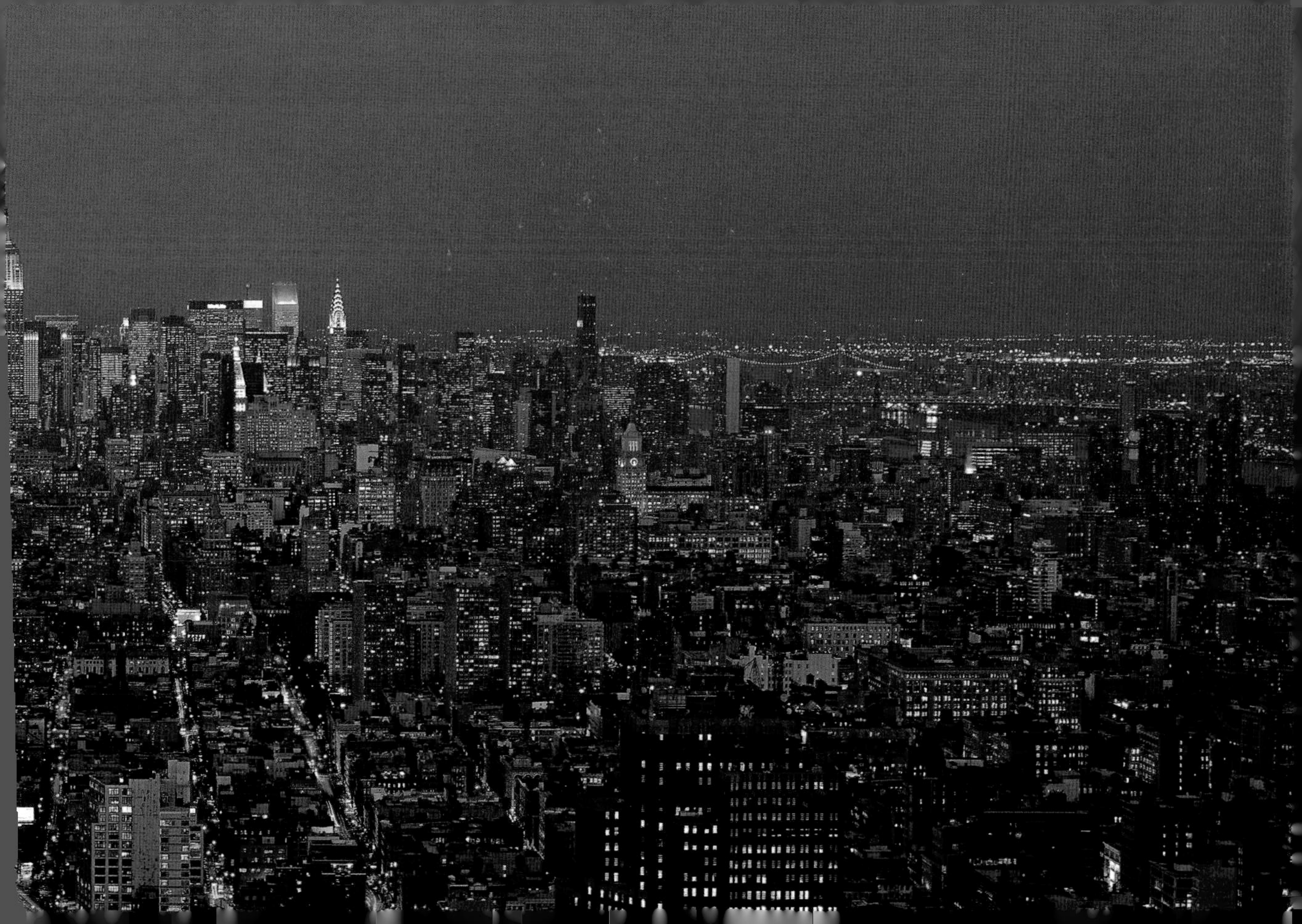

BAEFER

For my son Jack

a fifth-generation New Yorker

FOREWORD

GREAT CITIES HAVE DOMINATED THE GLOBE for millennia. Who could doubt that Plato, Socrates, and Aristotle made Athens the intellectual and philosophical center of the ancient world. Since then, a number of other magical places—especially Rome, Beijing, Edo (Tokyo), Constantinople, Venice, Madrid, Paris, and London—have in turn become the economic, political, and cultural center of civilization itself.

New York inherited the mantle of world leadership from London in 1917, when debt-plagued Great Britain had to turn to Wall Street to finance World War I. Certainly, by 1950, New York had become the locus of leadership for the world, when the establishment of the United Nations on the west side of Manhattan gave physical representation to a new kind of world order, in which the United States of America played the dominant role.

Gotham, of course, is not and never has been much like its European and Asian predecessors. Unlike them, it is not the national capital (the years between 1785 and 1790 were a brief exception). Unlike them, it never pointed to dozens of centuries old buildings as emblematic of its glory. And unlike them, it never drew much attention to its storied past.

Similarly, New York has long had a distinctiveness and a greatness that are all its own. Everyone has a particular way of defining the Hudson River metropolis. Some notice instantly and instinctively its unusual heterogeneity, which has been characteristic of the community since the Dutch first set up shop on Manhattan Island in 1625. Indeed, visitors to the seventeenth century settlement marveled that eighteen separate languages were spoken on its streets at a time when its total population was below one thousand. And in 2015, with more than 3 million foreign-born residents in the city, and over 200 languages spoken, New York remains the most diverse place on the planet, with half of its residents speaking a language other than English at home.

Other commentators point to New York's high population density and peculiar vertical shape, which can be noticed at once by glancing at the hundreds of skyscrapers that make the skyline recognizable everywhere. Still others point to its massive population, which is measurable not only by the 8,550,000 people who lived within its boundaries in 2015, but by the more than 15 million others who live in the adjacent counties.

Simply put, New York was the capital of the twentieth century and remains the capital of capitalism and the capital of the world. During its four hundred years, it has overcome virtually every challenge—from the burning of the city during the American Revolution to the horrific Draft Riots of 1863, to the financial collapse of Wall Street in 1929, to the attack on the Twin Towers in 2001.

Richard Berenholtz's *New York New York* captures the sweep, the diversity, the majesty, the energy, the beauty, the glitter, and even the madness of Gotham. From gargoyles to glass towers, from tranquil parks to chaotic Times Square, from details to panoramas, the pages that follow are as dynamic and glamorous as the city itself. This book can be examined with pleasure and profit by anyone interested in the human and physical story of what remains the most exciting city in the world.

KENNETH T. JACKSON

INTRODUCTION

I LOVE THIS CITY, FROM THE SMALLEST carving of an angel on a brownstone facade to the golden light reflecting off the glass wall of towering skyscrapers at sunrise, to the silhouetted miles of glittering skyline at dusk. New York is my birthplace, my workspace, my playground, and my home. I am of that increasingly rare breed known as "Native New Yorkers," and I wouldn't have it any other way.

The New York I love is a city of contradictions, filled with juxtapositions of old and new, past and present. Smooth steel and glass are the backdrop to carved stone gargoyles; a nineteenth-century church spire rises against the mirrored skin of a postmodern monolith; graffitied and postered walls form the bases of elegant cast iron structures from a past era. The architecturally innovative Guggenheim sits within blocks of the stately Metropolitan Museum of Art and the Smithsonian's Cooper Hewitt; restored Broadway show palaces stand amidst the flourescent glitz of a revitalized Times Square.

Yet, as New York was planned and developed, visionaries had the sense and foresight to dedicate areas for parks and open spaces, and nature was not forgotten. Central Park (with its Conservatory Garden, zoo, and playing fields), Riverside Park, and the exquisite Brooklyn Botanic and New York Botanical gardens are just a few of the protected natural grounds that make up the peaceful center of our active enclave of boroughs. This diverse palette of landscapes and vistas offer us sanctuaries from the noise and confinement of the surrounding concrete canyons.

Still, it is those very canyons that I find most compelling. When I walk this city, I delight in looking skyward. Admiring the view from below, I marvel at the sheer scale and expression of what mankind has chosen to create. From above, New York is yet another city altogether. Standing on the roof of a tall building, looking down over the endless expanse of steel, stone and glass, I can survey the chaotic criss-crossing of people and traffic from an unexpectedly quiet perch.

Whatever my vantage point, I watch with anticipation the continuous changes to the city, which is forever growing and reinventing itself as reflected in the seemingly endless alteration of the skyline. Time has shown that these changes are not always desirable, or for the best. We have lost some of the greatest architecture ever created—including the original Penn Station—through the shortsightedness of politicians and developers. These losses have taught us the value of preserving what we can of the fragile and irreplaceable buildings and monuments that form the link between then and now. We have also seen the skyline of one of the greatest cities on earth, and the lives of those who live and work there, violently and forever changed in a matter of moments through a senseless act of terrorism. I have taken the photographs in this book over the course of the last thirty-five years. They include the buildings and skylines that were, as well as those that exist today, for both the present and the past define the soul of our city.

New York City continues to provide an endless and rapidly changing source of inspiration for my work. I can go back to the same location countless times, and the light and conditions will never be the same. There is always something new to see that was not there before. I hope the photographs in this book will inspire both long-time residents as well as first-time visitors to look more closely at New York and to discover places and details they may have overlooked or taken for granted. We are never too young or too old to be surprised, and New York, if nothing else, is a city full of surprises.

RICHARD BERENHOLTZ

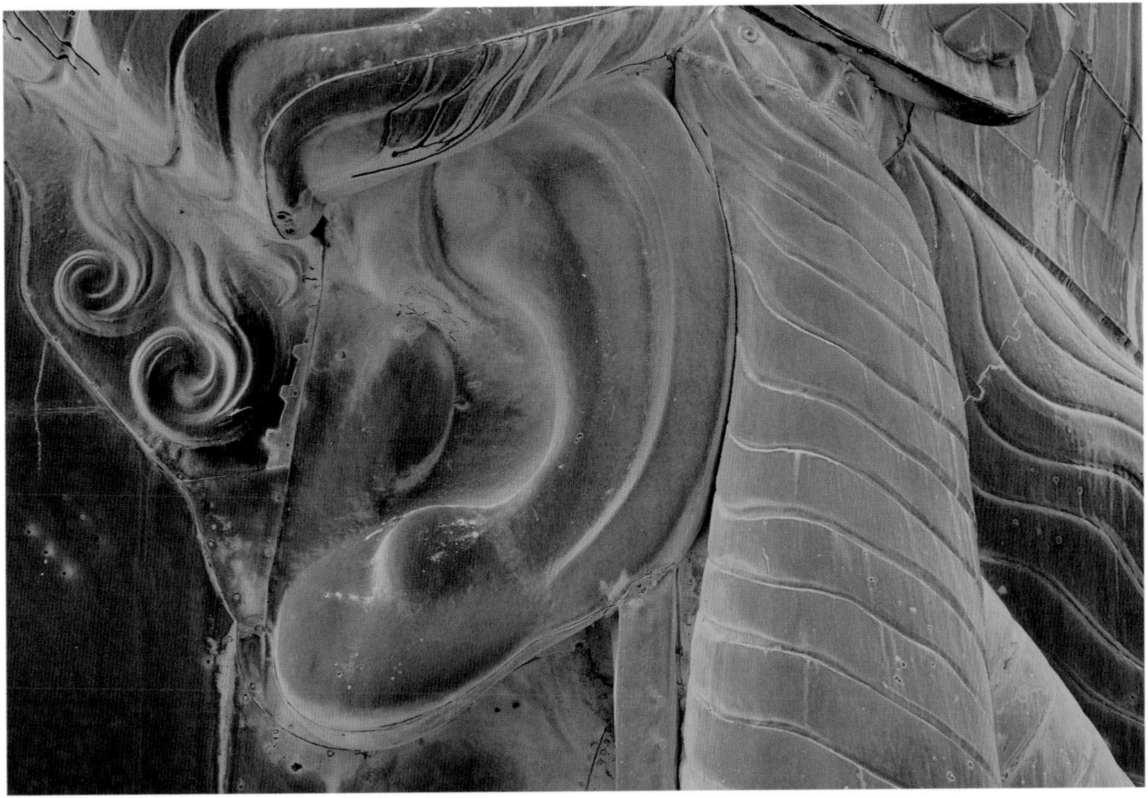

28

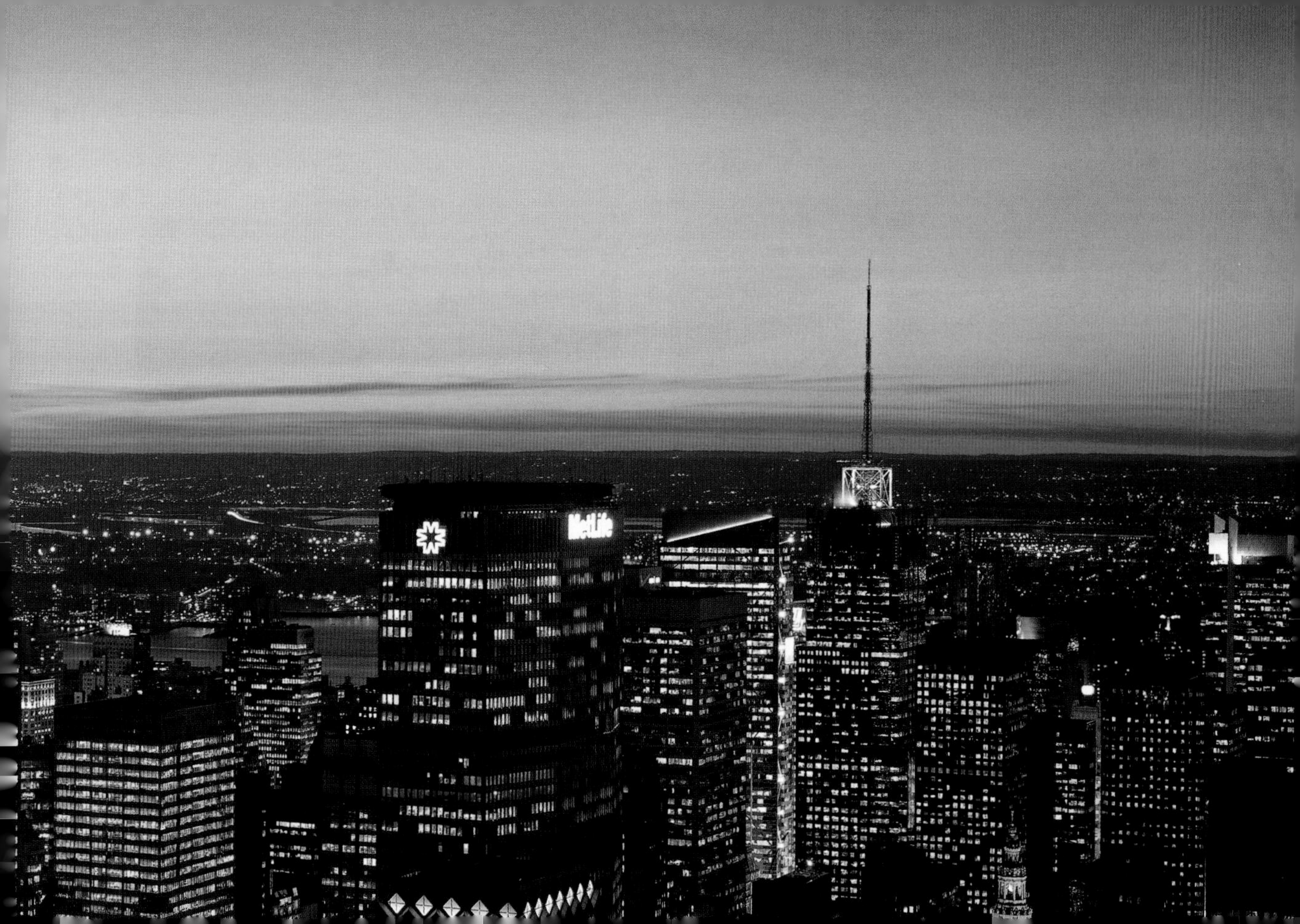
MetLife

DIRECTORY
25
43

GRAND CENTRAL
TERMINAL

NEW HAVEN LINE DEPARTURES
INFORMATION
TIME TRK DESTINATION REMARKS
RTURES
SUBWAY SHUTTLE
42ND STREET

WAITING ROOM
NORTH BALCONY
45TH STREET

43

12
1
2
3
4
5
6
7
8
9
10
11

P.D.

21
21
YVES
JOHN

THIS HORSE
DOES NOT
MOVE UP
AND DOWN

CNN

78

McGraw Rotunda

SOLOMON R GUGGENHEIM

ST AVGVSTINE
SAINT AIDAN

ST PAUL
MOSES

RADIO CITY
MUSIC HALL

ADIO CITY Music Hall RADIO CITY
HANKS ITS EMPLOYEES NOV 23 & 24 AT THE 60TH ANNIVERSARY RADIO CITY CHRISTMAS SPECTACULAR

THE DESERT
MASTER.COM OR 877-250-2929
AT LARGE
CHICAGO
THE MUSICAL
TELECHARGE.COM/CHICAGO or 212-239-6200
PRISCILLA QUEEN OF THE DESERT
the musical
CHANGE TODAY
MONEY EXCHANGE
TIMES SQUARE VISITOR CENTER
TIMES SQUARE VISITOR CENTER
McDonald's
OPEN 24 HOURS
McDonald's Restaurant
WHERE MAXIMUM PERFORMANCE LIVES
maxell
www.maxell.com
FRIDAYS
WINNER! 2010 TONY AWARD BEST MUSICAL
MEMPHIS
YOU ALREADY KNOW YOU'RE GONNA LOVE IT!
MAMMA MIA!
POLICE

EXCLUSIVE LIMITED EDITION
RÉMY
FACEBOOK.COM/REMYMARTIN
Hankook
driving emotion
Kodak
Kodak
SO KODAK
ST-PIERRE
SAT. APRIL
CLEARCHANNEL
Bank of America
MARQUIS
WONDERLAND
THE LION KING
TDK
SONY

SAMUELS

PAY AT REGISTER
EXIT
NOTICE
Coca-Cola

END TOMBS RIOT,
FREE HOSTAGES

THE COOPER UNION

&
BISCUITS
FIRST PRECINCT
POLICE MEETING
TUESDAY APRIL-30
AT
ST. ANTHONY'S
GYM-143 THOMPSON
7:30 PM.
EVERYONE IS
INVITED
BRING ALL YOUR
POLICE PROBLEMS
Anthony Dapolito
YES WE'RE
OPEN
VESUVIO BAKERY

VESUVIO
BAKERY
160-162
FIRST PRECINCT
POLICE MEETING
TUESDAY APRIL-30
AT
ST. ANTHONY'S
GYM-143 THOMPSON
7:30 PM.
EVERYONE IS
INVITED
BRIBG ALL YOUR
POLICE PROBLEMS

140

Home
for
your

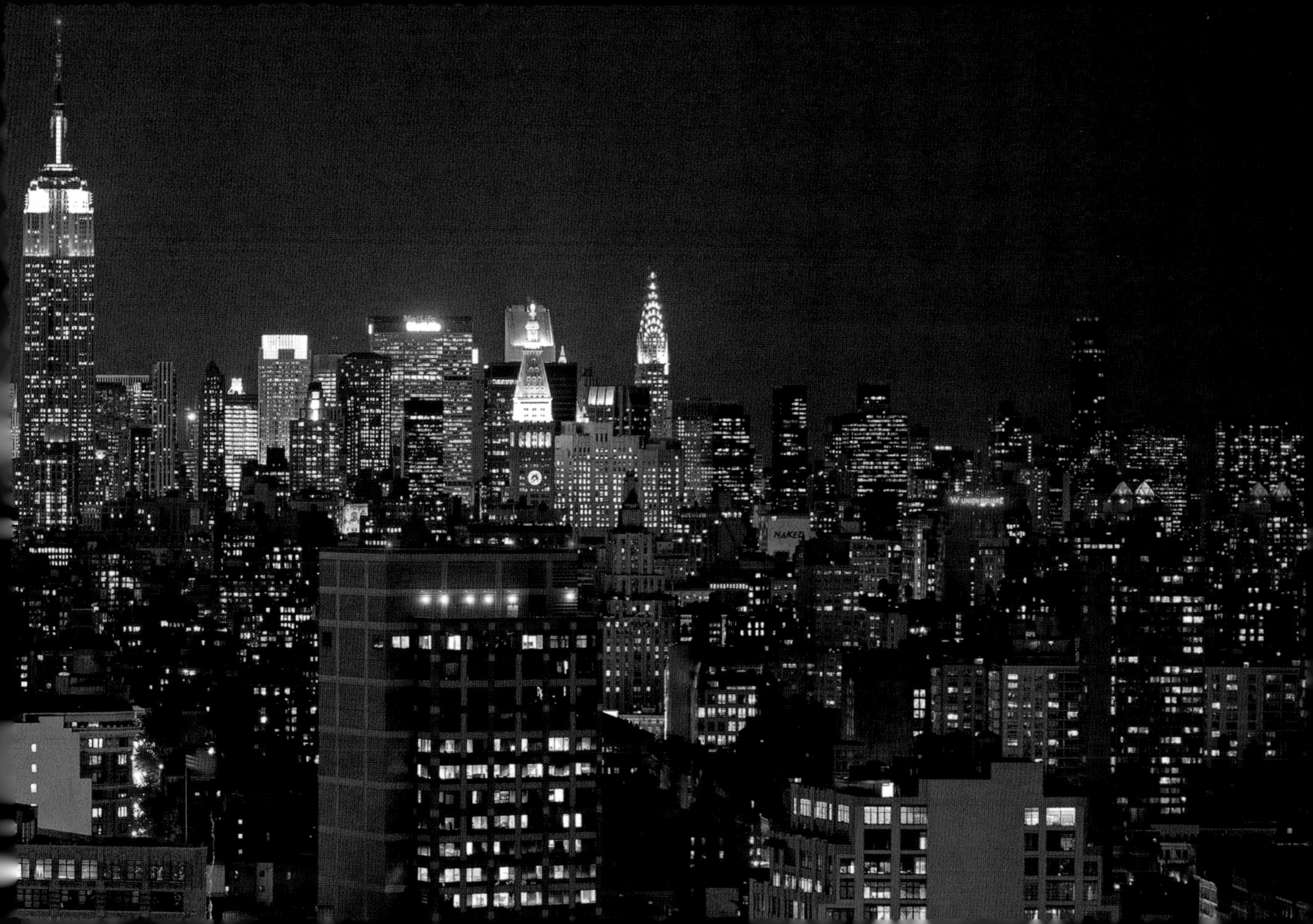
W UNION SQUARE
NAKED

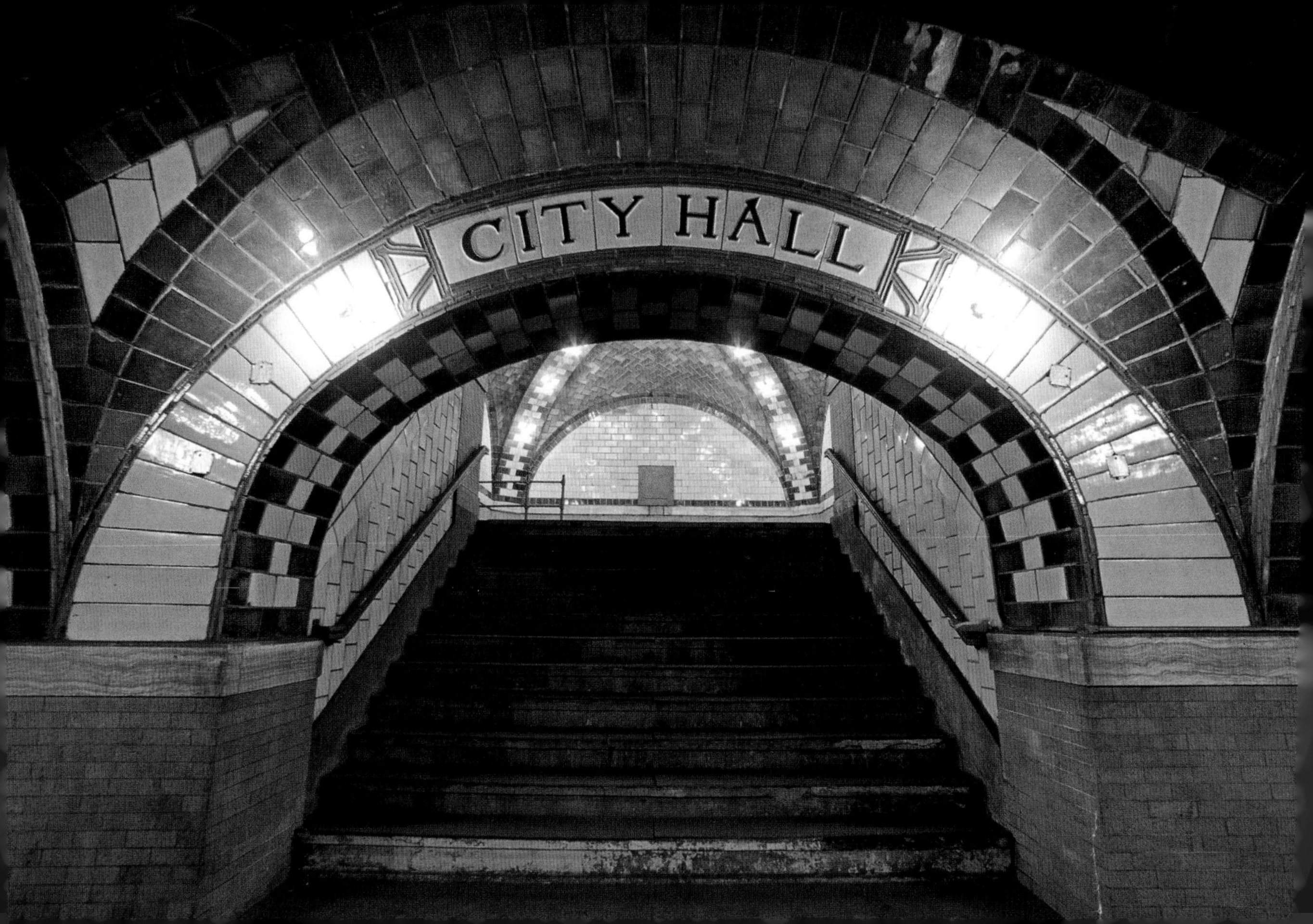
CITY HALL

BOROUGH HALL
IBH
IBH

大明神

ASTROLAND
CYCLO

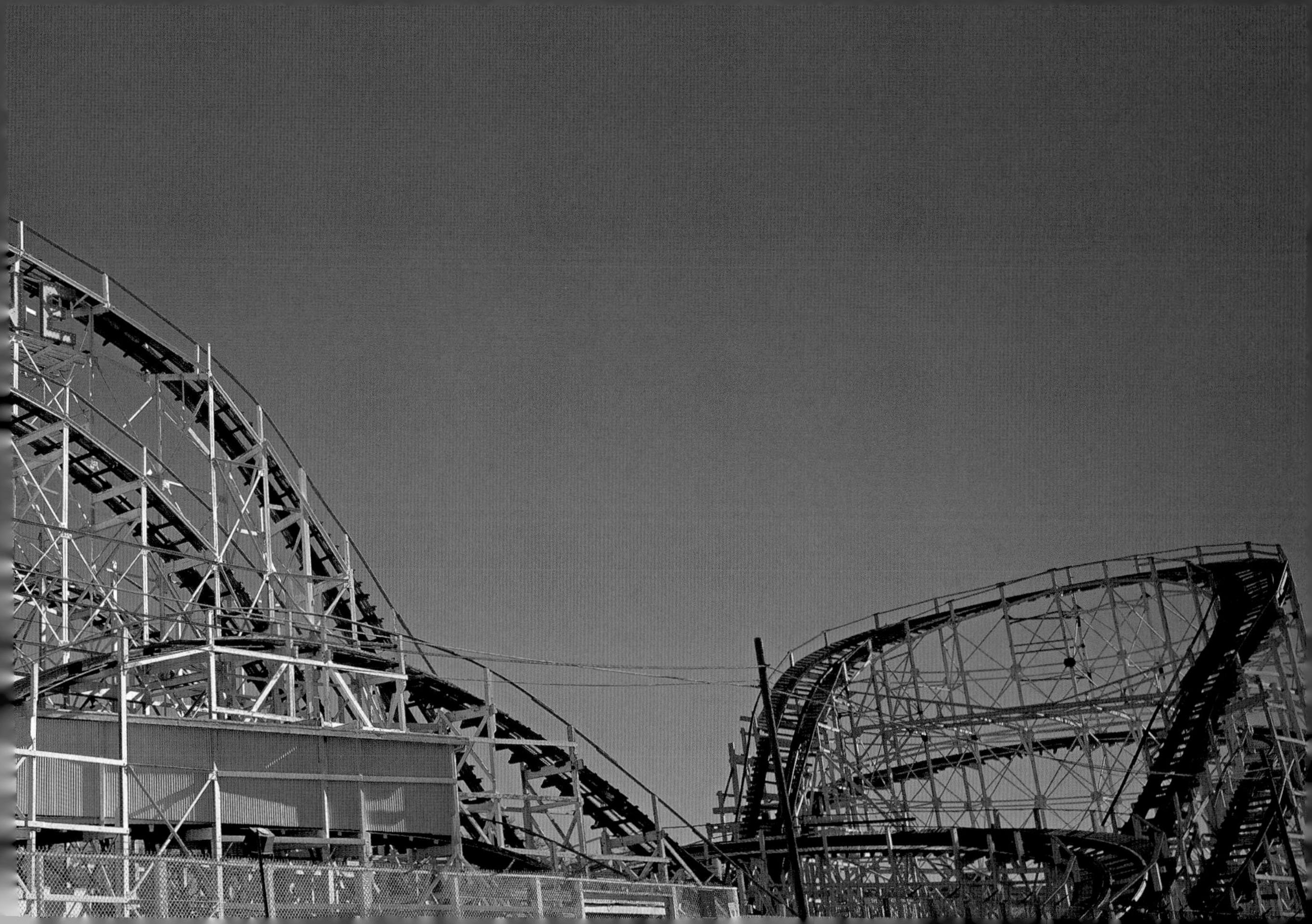

YANKEE

STADIUM

MetLife

MetLife

MetLife

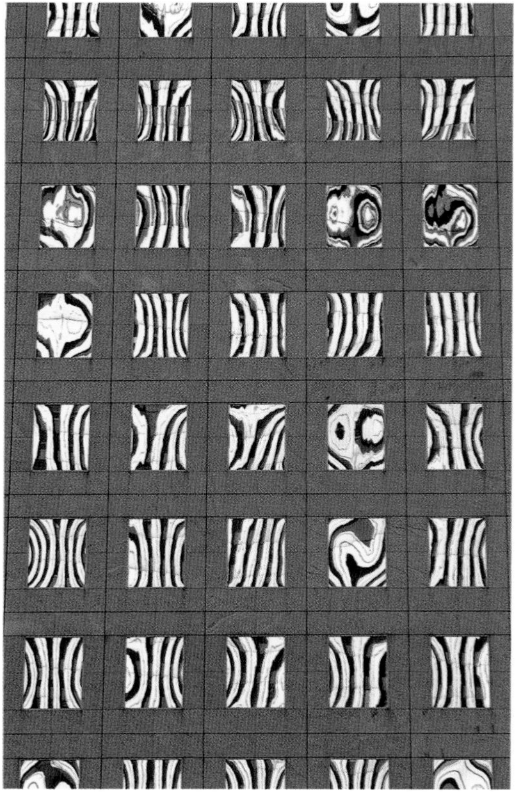

FIRE LANE
BUS
BUS

FIRE LANE
BUS

AVENUE
BUILDING

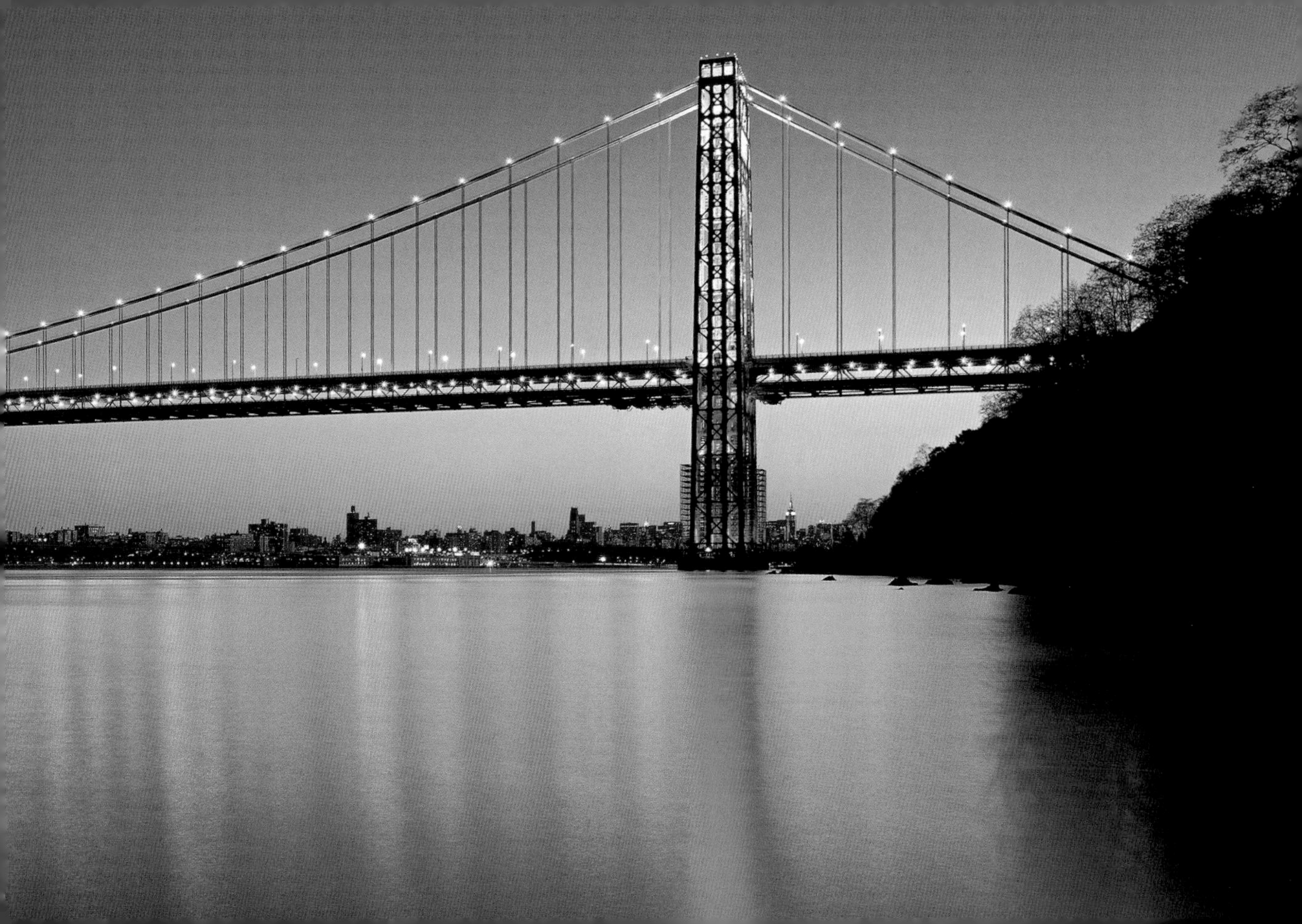

CONTAINER CAFE

210

NEW YORK STOCK EXCHANGE

213

INTERNATIONAL
TELEPHONE AND TELEGRAPH
CORPORATION

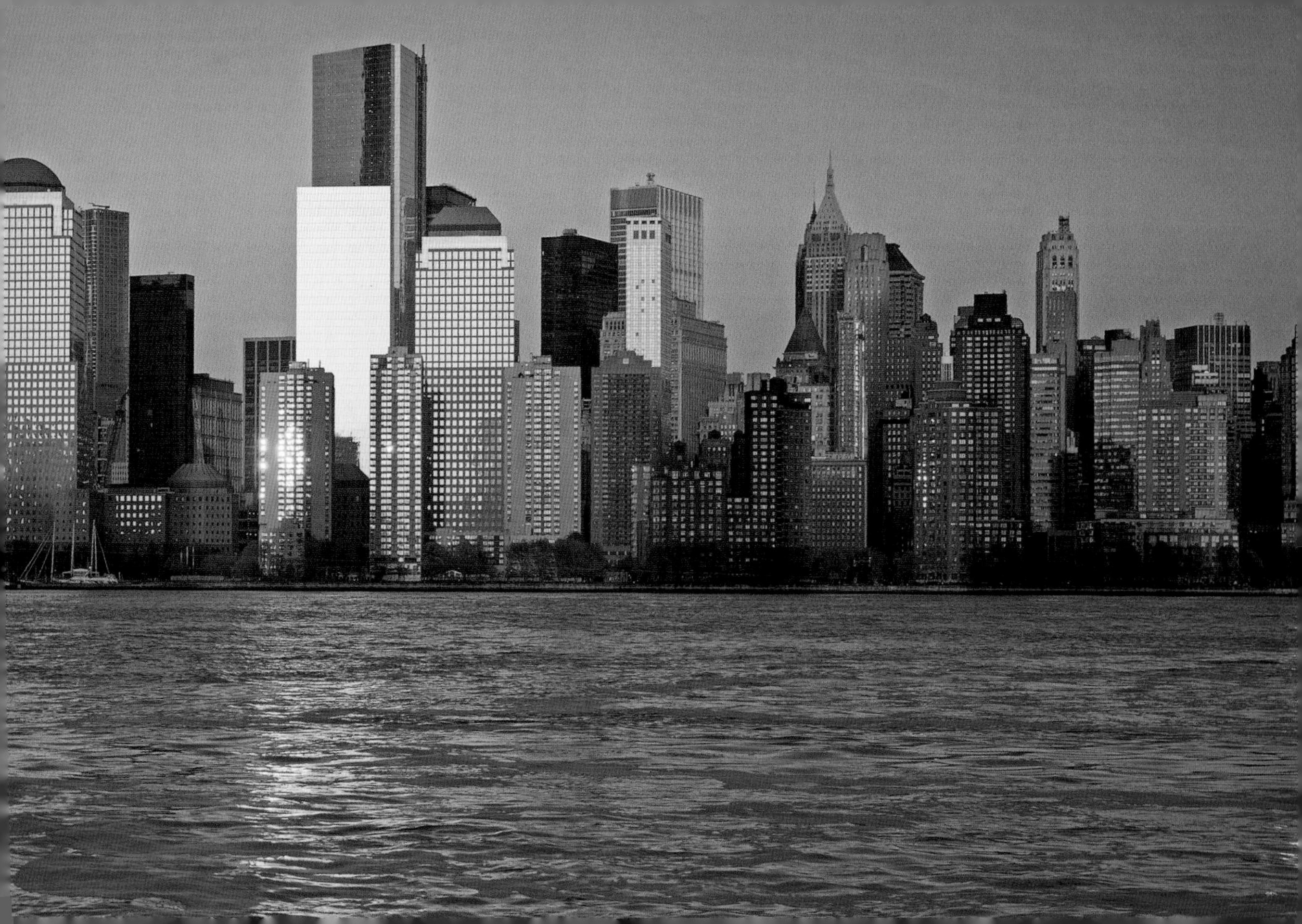

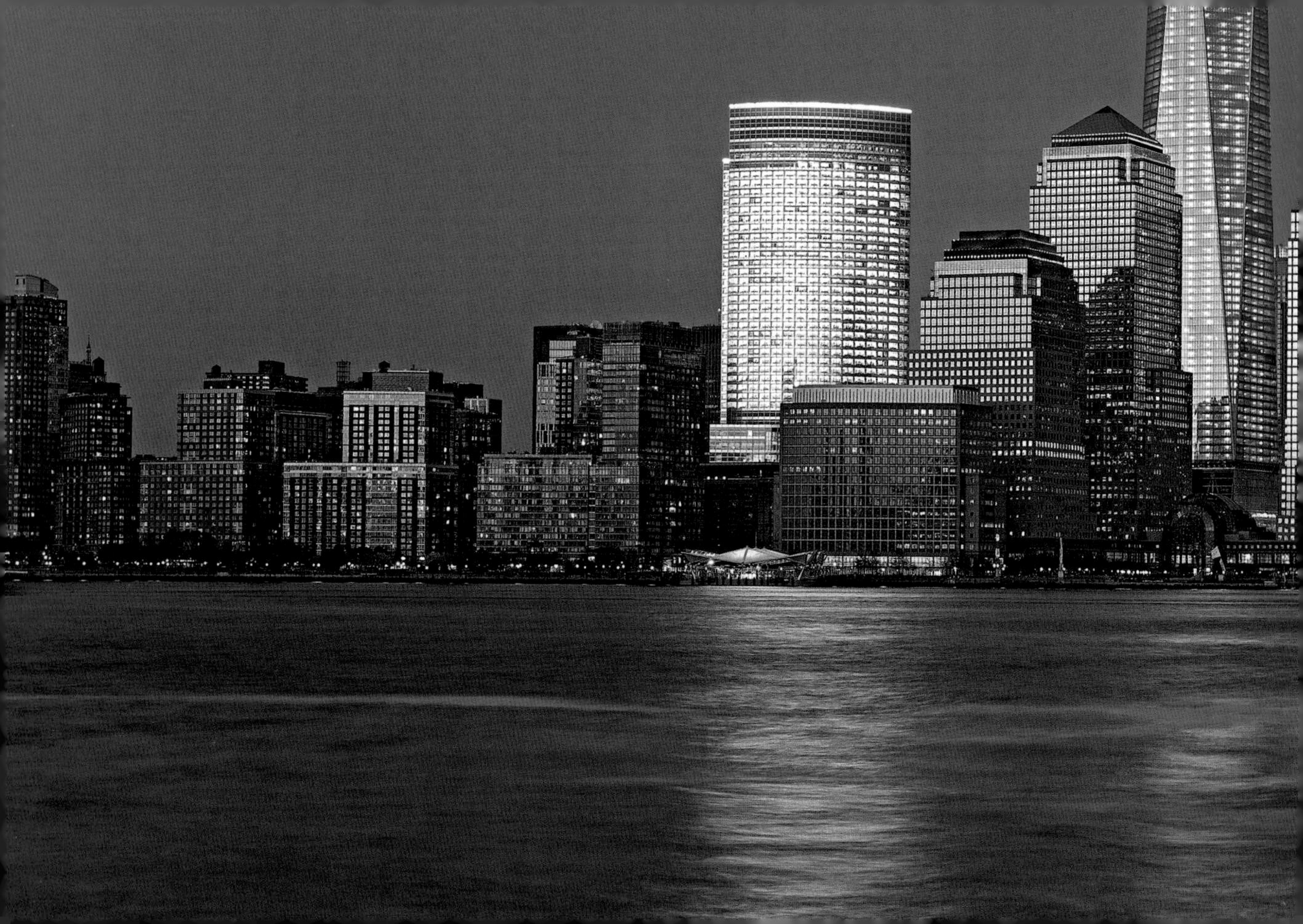

INDEX

36–37 Chrysler Building lobby. *Page 34, left to right*: ceiling mural detail (Edward Trumbull); elevator doors; and ceiling mural detail.

38–39 Exterior of Grand Central Terminal (Warren and Wetmore, 1913) with Hyatt Hotel and Chrysler Building in background.

40–41 Interior of Grand Central Terminal.

42–43 Ceiling details in Grand Central Terminal.

44–45 Clock at Grand Central Terminal (Jules Alexis Coutan, 1929). *Page 43, clocks, clockwise from top left*: Helmsley Building (Warren and Wetmore, 1929); building on Avenue C; building on East 4th St.; and Central Savings Bank (York & Sawyer, 1928).

46–47 *Clocks, from left to right*: Schwarzenbach Building; 52nd Police Precinct, Bronx (1906); and Tiffany's (Harry Frederick Metzler, 1853).

48–49 *Left to right*: Exterior of the 21 Club (1929); detail of Macy's (1902); and exterior of Saks Fifth Avenue (Starrett & Van Vleck, 1924).

50–51 Terra-cotta ornamentation on Fred F. French Building (Sloan & Robertson, 1927). Lee Lawrie's Atlas (1937), Olympic Tower (Skidmore, Owings & Merrill, 1976) and St. Patrick's Cathedral (James Renwick Jr. & William Rodrique, 1888).

52–53 Ceiling painting by José Maria Sert in 30 Rockefeller Plaza (G.E. Building). Rockefeller Center (Reinhard & Hofmeister; Corbett, Harrison & MacMurray; Raymond Hood; Godley & Fouilhoux, 1940).

54–55 Details from Rockefeller Center.

56–57 Midtown Manhattan at night.

58–59 Prometheus statue by Paul Manship (1934), Rockefeller Center. Promenade at Christmas, Rockefeller Center.

60–61 Bow Bridge,Central Park (Calvert Vaux, 1859).

62–63 "Angel of the Waters" at the Bethesda Fountain, Central Park (Emma Stebbins, 1873). *Page 61, clockwise from top left*: the pond in Central Park; the Gapstow Bridge (Howard Caudwell, 1896); Central Park landscapes.

64–65 Allée of crab apples in the Conservatory Garden, Central Park.

66–67 Untermyer Fountain with bronze by Walter Schott in the North Garden of the Conservatory Garden (1947).

68–69 Frances Hodgson Burnett Memorial Fountain (sculptor Bessie Potter Vonnoh, 1937) in the South Garden of the Conservatory Garden.

70–71 Bow Bridge, Central Park, with Central Park West in background.

72–73 Friedsam Carousel carved by Solomon Stern and Harry Goldstein (1908; transferred from Coney Island to Central Park in 1951).

74–75 *Left*: Aerial view of The Plaza Hotel (Henry Janeway Hardenbergh, 1907) and Grand Army Plaza (Carrère and Hastings, 1916) near Central Park. *Right*: Central Park South at sunrise and at dusk.

76–77 Looking north over Central Park in autumn.

78, 81 Metropolitan Museum of Art (Calvert Vaux & Jacob Wrey Mould, 1880). *Page 78*: Main entrance facade and the Temple of Dendur in the Sackler Wing. *Page 81*: American Wing (Roche, Dinkeloo and Assoc., 1980).

79–80 Metropolitan Museum of Art's Great Hall (Richard Morris Hunt, 1902).

82–83 *Left to right*: Museum of Modern Art (Philip S. Goodwin and Edward D. Stone, 1939); Cooper Hewitt Museum (Babb, Cook & Willard, 1903); and The Frick Collection's formal garden (Russell Page, 1977).

84–85 The Cuxa Cloister, Fort Tyron Park (reconstructed from a 12th-century Benedictine monastery in the Pyrenees, 1925).

86–87 Interior and exterior of Grant's Tomb (John H. Duncan, 1897).

88–89 New York Public Library (Carrère and Hastings, 1911). *Left*: Lion Statue by E. C. Potter. *Right*: McGraw Rotunda.

90–91 Rose Planetarium, The Museum of Natural History (James Stewart Polshek, 2000).

92–93 Exterior views and interior of the Solomon R. Guggenheim Museum (Frank Lloyd Wright, 1959).

94–95 Solomon R. Guggenheim Museum.

96–97 Building details.

98–99 Exterior of Riverside Church (Allen & Collens, Henry C. Pelton, 1930).

100–101 Interior of Riverside Church.

102, 105 St. John the Divine (Heins & Lafarge, Ralph Adams Cram, 1941). *Page 102*: Main entrance facade. *Page 105*: Angel detail.

103–104 Interior of St. John the Divine.

106–107 *Left to right*: Tops of Riverside Church; Central Synagogue (Henry Ferbach, 1872); and Episcopal Church of the Holy Trinity (J. Stewart Barney, 1897). Interior of Central Synagogue.

108–109 Williamsburg Savings Bank, "Cathedral of Thrift," Brooklyn (Halsey, McCormack & Helmer, 1929). The elevator lobby in the Waldorf Astoria (Schultze and Weaver, 1931).

110–111 *Left to right*: University Club Library (McKim, Mead and White, 1899); The Pierpont Morgan Library (Charles McKim, 1906); and the lobby ceiling of the Woolworth Building (Cass Gilbert, 1913).

112–113 Radio City Music Hall (Edward Durrell Stone, 1932).

114–115 Women's and Men's Lounges designed by Donald Deskey, Radio City Music Hall.

116–117 Times Square, looking south between Broadway and Seventh Avenue.

118–119 Lincoln Center at dusk (Harrison & Abramovitz; Philip Johnson; Eero Saarinen; Pietro Belluschi; and others, 1969).

120–121 Airline Diner (Jackson Hole Wyoming), Astoria, Queens (1954). McSorley's Old Ale House, East Village (1854).

122–123 41 Cooper Square (Thom Mayne, Morphosis, 2009), The Cooper Union for the Advancement of Science and Art; The New Museum of Contemporary Art (Sejima + Nishizawa/SANAA, 2007); and the High Line, looking south from 13th Street and north from 14th Street.

124, 129 The Empire State Building and Midtown Manhattan, loking south at dawn and dusk.

125–128 View of Manhattan from Long Island City, Queens, at dusk.

130–131 Vesuvio Bakery, SoHo.

132–133 The Puck Building, SoHo.

134–135 Street facade, SoHo. Apartment building detail, East 14th Street.

136–137 Railing at the Players Club, Gramercy Park (Stanford White, 1889). Washington Square townhouses (1833).

138–139 Bayard-Condict Building on Bleecker Street (Louis Sullivan, 1899).

140–141 Building ornamentation, East 16th Street. Railing at the Dakota on Central Park West (Henry J. Hardenberch, 1884).

142–143 *Left to right*: brownstones, Upper West Side; Striver's Row, Harlem (James Brown Lad; Bruce Price; Clarence S. Luce; and McKim, Mead & White, 1891); and brownstones, Upper West Side.

144–145 The "Gargoyle Building," Upper West Side. Pomander Walk, Upper West Side (King & Campbell, 1922).

146, 149 Building details, *from left to right*: Upper West Side YMCA; Pythian Temple (Thomas W. Lamb, 1927); and Pythian Temple.

147–48 Original Audubon Theater and Ballroom (Thomas W. Lamb, 1912).

150–151 Building details. *Page 150, clockwise from top left*: Lafayette Street; West End Avenue; Columbus Avenue; and 8th Avenue. *Page 151*: Park Avenue.

152–153 View of Midtown Manhattan skyline looking north in late afternoon and at dusk.

154–155 View of Midtown Manhattan skyline looking north at night.

156–157 Subway stations. *Left*: original City Hall station (1904). *Right*: Borough Hall station (1933) in Brooklyn.

158–159 The Japanese Garden at the Brooklyn Botanic Garden (Takeo Shiota, 1915).

160–161 *Page 160*: Japanese Garden footbridge and walking path. *Page 161*: Soldiers' and Sailors' Memorial Arch at the Grand Army Plaza (John H. Duncan, 1892) and the Bailey Fountain at the Grand Army Plaza (Eugene Savage, 1932).

162–163 The Cyclone rollercoaster at Surf Avenue, Coney Island (1927).

164–165 Yankee Stadium, Bronx (Populous, 2009).

166–167 Enid Annenberg Haupt Conservatory at the New York Botanical Garden, Bronx (William R. Cobb, 1902).

168–171 Midtown Manhattan skyline featuring The New York Times Building (Renzo Piano, 2007); 4 Times Square (Fox & Fowle Architects, 2000); and the Bank of America Tower. (COOKFOX Architects, 2009).

172–173 Exterior and interior of the Jacob K. Javitz Convention Center (I. M. Pei and Partners, 1986).

174–175 Building reflections. *Page 174, clockwise from top left*: the Fuller Building; Lower Manhattan; Midtown; and the "Lipstick Building" in Midtown. *Page 175, left to right*: A World Trade Center Tower in the windows of the World Financial Center; Lower Manhattan.

176–177 Avenue of the Americas, Midtown.

178–179 Looking up from Broadway in Lower Manhattan. *Page 179, clockwise from top left*: Avenue of the Americas; Avenue of the Americas; Third Avenue in Midtown; and East 53rd Street.

180–181 *Left to right*: Time Warner Center (Skidmore, Owings, & Merrill, 2003); Hearst Tower (Foster + Partners, 2006); and Bloomberg Tower/One Beacon Court (Pelli Clarke Pelli Architects, 2005).

182–183 *Left to right*: IAC Building (Frank Gehry, 2007); 100 11th Avenue (Jean Nouvel, 2009); and New York by Gehry building (Frank Gehry, 2011).

184–185 Towers of 15 Park Row (R. H. Robertson, 1899) with the Transportation Building (York & Sawyer, 1927) and Woolworth Building.

186–187 Building tops. *Left to right*: Original G.E. Building (Cross and Cross, 1931); New York Life Insurance Building (Cass Gilbert, 1928); Fuller Building (Walker and Gillette, 1929); and the Police Building (Hoppin and Koen, 1909).

188–189 Building tops. *Left to right*: The Bryant Park Hotel, original American Radiator Building (Hood and Fouilhoux, 1924); Ansonia Hotel (Paul E. M. Duboy, 1904); Flatiron Building, original Fuller Building (Daniel H. Burnham and Co., 1902); and Citicorp Center (Hugh Stubbins and Assoc., 1978).

190–191 Building tops. *Left to right*: Crown Building (Warren and Wetmore, 1921); Met Life Tower (LeBrun and Sons, 1909); original Paramount Theater Building (Rapp and Rapp, 1927); and the Woolworth Building (Cass Gilbert, 1913).

192, 197 *Page 192*: Queensboro "59th Street" Bridge (1909) from Long Island City; the Manhattan Bridge (1909). *Page 197*: Williamsburg Bridge (1903) from Williamsburg, Brooklyn; Brooklyn Bridge (1883) from DUMBO in Brooklyn.

193–196 The Whitestone Bridge (1939) from the Bronx at dusk.

198–199 The Manhattan Bridge.

200–201 George Washington Bridge (1931) from the Palisades, New Jersey.

202–203 *Left to right*: The George Washington Bridge from Manhattan; the Manhattan Bridge from Brooklyn Heights; and the Verrazano Narrows Bridge from Staten Island (1964).

204–205 The Brooklyn Bridge.

206–207 The Brooklyn Bridge from Brooklyn Heights.

208–209 Broad Street in Lower Manhattan. South Street Seaport (1984).

210–211 Art deco lobby of the Bank of New York on Wall Street, which was the original Irving Trust Co. (Ralph Walker, 1932). New York Stock Exchange at Broad Street, (George B. Post, 1903).

212–213 *Left to right*: 90 West Street (Cass Gilbert, 1907); and exterior and interior of Trinity Church (Richard Upjohn, 1846).

214–215 *Left to right*: Building door, Financial District; Art

238

ACKNOWLEDGMENTS

A special thank-you to my family and friends
for their encouragement and support:
My parents—Marjorie and Harry
Jim Berenholtz, Nanette Cohen, Gerald Kantor, John Steffy,
and Bonnie Webster.

I also wish to express my gratitude and appreciation
to my friends at Rizzoli and Welcome Enterprises:
Charles Miers and John Brancati,
who shared the vision and said, "Yes!";
Lena Tabori, without whom this book could never have been done;
Katrina Fried, for her tireless efforts; and Gregory Wakabayashi,
the best designer I've had the privilege of working with.

R. B.

Original edition first published in the United States of America in 2002 by
Rizzoli International Publications, Inc.
300 Park Avenue South, New York, NY 10010
www.rizzoliusa.com

Publisher: Charles Miers
Editor: Jessica Fuller

Produced by Welcome Enterprises, Inc.
6 West 18th Street, New York, NY 10011
www.welcomeenterprisesinc.com

Project Directors: Katrina Fried and Lena Tabori
Art Director: Gregory Wakabayashi

ISBN: 978-0-8478-5990-0

Library of Congress Catalog Control Number: 2016957219

2017 2018 2019 2020 / 10 9 8 7 6 5 4 3 2 1
PRINTED IN CHINA

For more information about the photographer and to purchase original prints please visit: www.photographynewyork.com